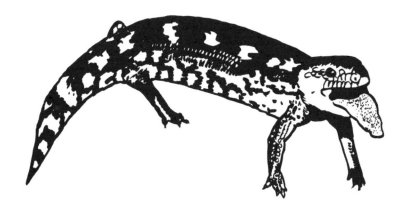

Australian Reptiles
Colour and Learn

When threatened this large skink sticks out its blue-black tongue to ward off danger. It occurs across a wide area of Australia and has many different names including bobtail, stumpy-tail, sleepy lizard, boggi and pinecone lizard.

Shingleback

This beautiful snake only lives in a small area of north Queensland, where it blends in perfectly with the green foliage in its rainforest habitat. Young pythons of this species are bright yellow for their first year or so before turning emerald green.

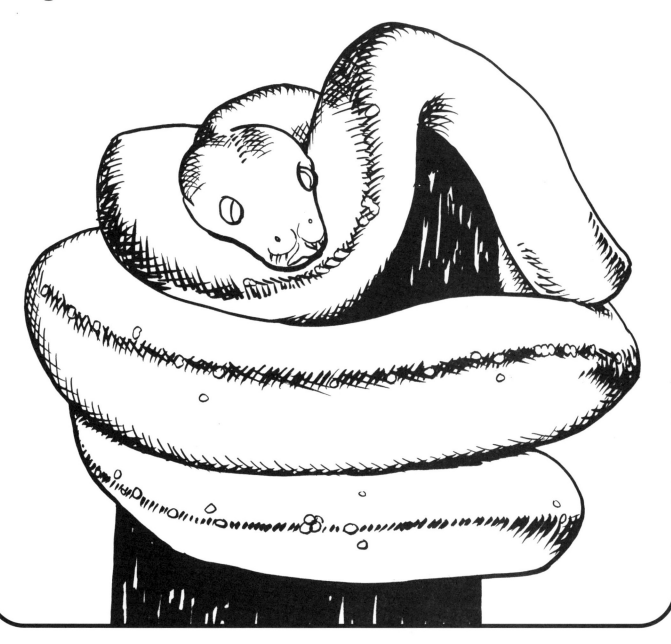

Green Python

Living in the arid interior of Australia this species is also known as the barking gecko because of the call that it uses in defence. It is the most widespread of ten similar species of knob-tailed geckos which are found all over Australia.

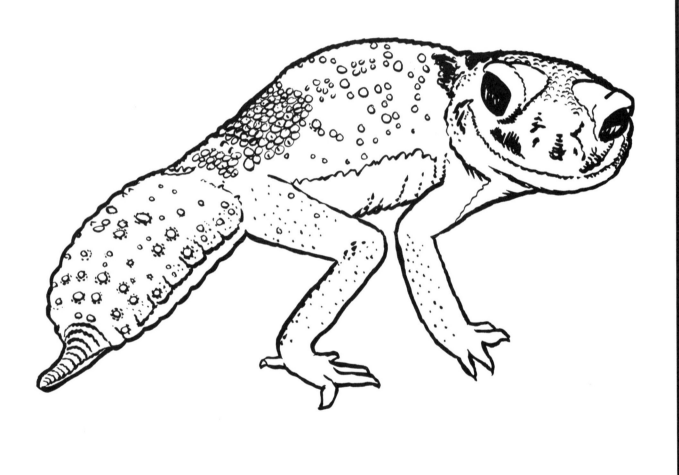

Smooth Knob-tailed Gecko

Measuring about 60 centimetres in length this medium-sized monitor can be found in central and north-west Australia. On its body the pale spots with dark centres – known as ocelli – help the lizard to camouflage itself among rocks and vegetation.

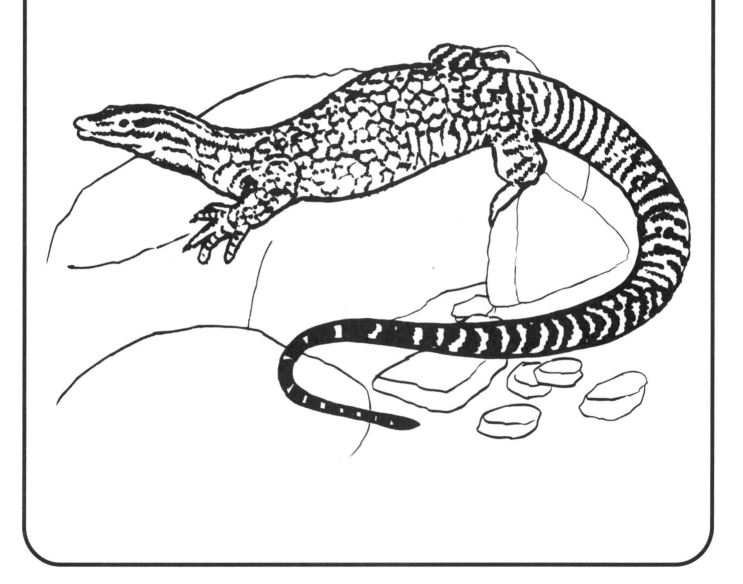

Spiny-tailed Monitor

This beautiful-looking member of the snapping turtle family lives only in one river system in New South Wales. It is very rare and declining and is threatened with extinction.

George's Turtle

With its slender snout this crocodile is generally considered to be not dangerous to humans. It feeds on prey such as fish, frogs and birds, and lives in freshwater rivers and billabongs in northern Australia.

Freshwater Crocodile

The spectacular 'beard' is formed of spiny scales. This is one of the most familiar lizards in Australia because it often occurs in and around towns and cities, from Cairns down to Adelaide, whilst it is also popular in captivity.

Eastern Bearded Dragon

One of Australia's most lethal snakes, this species is capable of delivering large quantities of venom. It has a distinctive broad body with pale and dark stripes and is found in eastern and southern Australia.

Common Death Adder

After hatching from an egg buried on a sandy beach these turtles head straight for the sea. They spend their entire lives wandering the oceans, with only the females occasionally coming ashore in order to lay clutches of eggs on the same beach where they hatched.

Green Turtle

With a spectacular spiny crest on its head and back this dragon looks like a miniature dinosaur. It is found only in a few small areas of rainforest in Queensland, where it can be hard to spot amongst the leaves and stems.

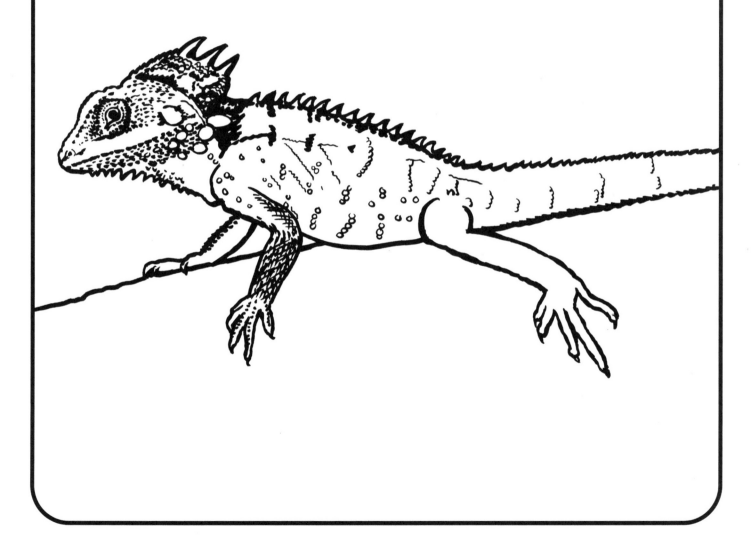

Boyd's Forest Dragon

This smart-looking striped python can grow to more than 2 metres in length. It inhabits the arid centre of Australia and feeds mostly on other reptiles, including on venomous snakes.

Woma

Measuring up to 2.4 metres in length, this huge monitor lizard is almost comparable in size to the notorious Komodo Dragon of Indonesia. The net-like pattern on the Perentie's head and neck is known as reticulation.

Perentie

These highly venomous snakes are very variable in pattern with the 'tiger stripes' only present in some individuals, most frequently in juveniles, while many are plain brown or black.

Tiger Snake

Measuring a maximum of only 10 centimetres, this small and beautifully patterned gecko lives in hollows and crevices on rocky outcrops in the northernmost part of Northern Territory.

Northern Marbled Velvet Gecko

This large lizard can be found in woodlands and forests in eastern Australia. The female Lace Monitor lays her eggs in a termite mound, either in a tree or on the ground.

Lace Monitor

These impressive dragons are familiar to many people as they often inhabit parks in towns and cities in eastern Australia. Invariably found close to water they are strong swimmers and will readily swim to safety if disturbed.

Eastern Water Dragon

Living in wetlands and swamps, this distinctive looking and dangerously venomous snake feeds mainly on frogs. It has declined recently due to feeding on introduced Cane Toads, which are poisonous.

Red-bellied Black Snake

With its remarkably shaped tail and flattened body, and an intricate pattern of blotches on its skin, this gecko blends in perfectly against a background of lichen-covered rainforest tree trunks. It is found only in a tiny area of Queensland.

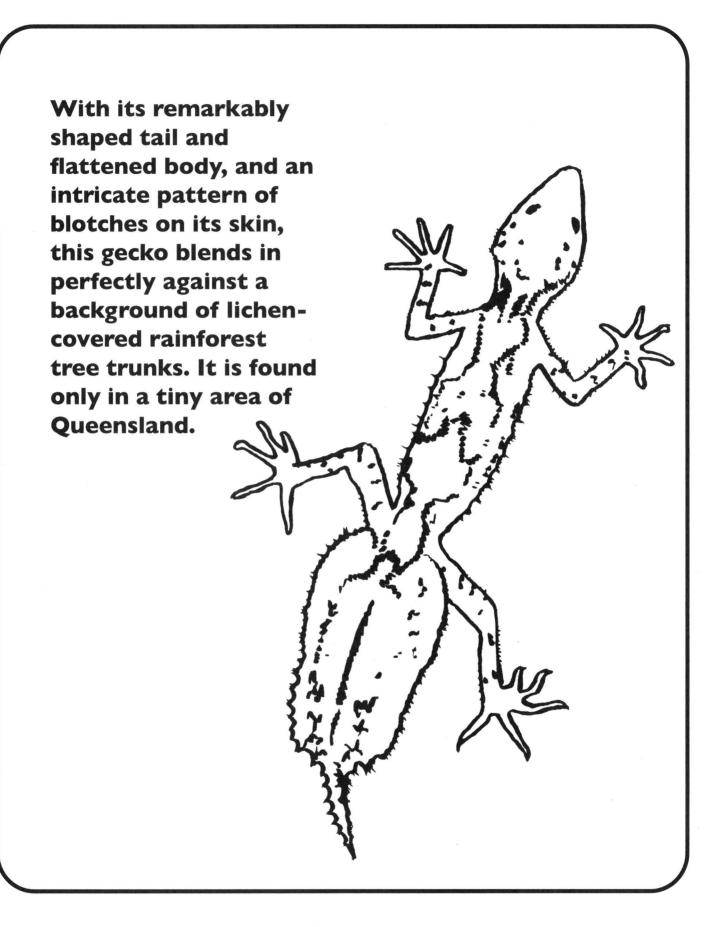

Northern Leaf-tailed Gecko

Widespread across eastern Australia, this striking-looking turtle is found in a variety of freshwater habitats including rivers and lakes. Individuals can sometimes be found wandering on land far from water looking for new habitats, especially after rain.

Eastern Long-necked Turtle

This large skink is found mainly in Victoria and Tasmania, while very similar species occur all over Australia. If threatened the lizard will stick out its large blue tongue and make a hissing sound to ward off potential danger.

Southern Blue-tongue

A burrowing predator that feeds exclusively on blind snakes, the bandy bandy only ventures above ground at night. In defence it will twist and turn its body into curling loops.

Common Bandy Bandy

Growing up to 7 metres in length and feeding on large prey, this crocodile is the apex predator in coastal environments of northern Australia, where it is at home in rivers, lakes and the sea.

Saltwater Crocodile

Published in 2022 by Reed New Holland Publishers
Sydney • Auckland

Level 1, 178 Fox Valley Road, Wahroonga, NSW 2076, Australia
5/39 Woodside Avenue, Northcote, Auckland 0627, New Zealand

newhollandpublishers.com

A record of this book is held at the National Library of Australia.

ISBN 978 1 76079 464 4

Managing Director: Fiona Schultz
Publisher and Project Editor: Simon Papps
Designer and illustrator: Andrew Davies
Production Director: Arlene Gippert
Printed in China

10 9 8 7 6 5 4 3 2 1

Also available from Reed New Holland:
Australian Birds: Colour and Learn
ISBN 978 1 76079 426 2

Australian Wildlife: Colour and Learn
ISBN 978 1 76079 432 3

Australian Butterflies: Colour and Learn
ISBN 978 1 76079 465 1

Colour With Chris Humfrey's Awesome Australian Animals
ISBN 978 1 76079 424 8

Chris Humfrey's Awesome Australian Animals
ISBN 978 1 92554 670 5

A Complete Guide to Australian Reptiles
ISBN 978 1 92554 671 2

For details of hundreds of other Natural History titles see
newhollandpublishers.com

And keep up with Reed New Holland and New Holland Publishers on Facebook

 ReedNewHolland and NewHollandPublishers

 @newhollandpublishers